Nelson

Handwriting

Pupil Book 2

Unit	Handwriting	Pages
1	Revision of the unjoined script and the joins	2-3
2	Revision of e, s and f	4-5
3	Practice with poems and prose	6-9
4	Joining consonants	10-11
	ff, ll, ss	*10*
	scr, spl, spr, str	*11*
5	Vowel digraphs	12-13
6	Practice with all the joins	14-15
	Silent letters	*14*
	ch	*15*
7	Practice with verbs and adverbs	16-17
8	Practice with conjunctions	18-19
	and	*18*
	but	*19*
9	Questions and answers	20-21
10	Inverted commas	22-23
11	Writing with a slope	24-27
12	Vocabulary practice	28-29
	Synonyms	*28*
	Antonyms	*29*
13	Dictionary skills	30-31
	Alphabetical order	*30*
	Definitions	*31*
14	Speed writing	32-35
15	Drafting and editing	36-37
16	Print	38-41
17	Writing in ink	42-45
18	Writing letters	46-47
19	Check your writing	48

Nelson

Unit 1 — Revision of the unjoined script and the joins

Look at these letters and numerals.

Lower case letters

a b c d e f g h i j k l m n
o p q r s t u v w x y z

Capital letters

A B C D E F G H I J K L M N O P Q
R S T U V W X Y Z

Numerals

0 1 2 3 4 5 6 7 8 9

Copy the letters and numerals.
Check your writing against the page.

It is important to check that you are forming the letters and joins correctly.

Copy these patterns.

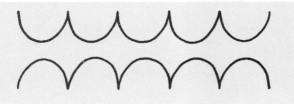

Set 1 letters: a c d e h i k l m n s t u
Set 2 letters: a c d e g i j m n o p q r s u v w x y
Set 3 letters: b f h k l t
Set 4 letters: f o r v w
Break letters: b g j p q x y z

Now practise the four joins.

The first join
Set 1 to Set 2

an co he ku te ag

The second join
Set 1 to Set 3

ch ib ul ck al et

The third join
Set 4 to Set 2

ws rm on we va fu

The fourth join
Set 4 to Set 3

ok fl wh ol ff

The break letters

band gate jar pencil
quite foxes yacht zebra

3

Unit 2 — Revision of e, s and f

The letters e, s and f need plenty of practice. Look at these joins to and from e, s and f.

e

After **Set 1** letters

ae de he le se ue

After **Set 4** letters

fe oe re ve we

Notice how e changes its shape, according to which kind of letter it follows.

s

After **Set 1** letters

as cs ks ms ts us

After **Set 4** letters

fs os rs vs ws

f

To f

af cf if mf of rf

From f

fe fl fm fn fu ft

Practise writing these letters and joins until you can form them easily and well.

4

The word *in* is a preposition. It tells us how one word relates to another.

These five <u>foxes</u> are <u>in</u> <u>boxes</u>.

● Write these sentences neatly, taking special care over the letters *e*, *s* and *f*.

1. Six sausages were under the grill.
2. My cat Fluff hid behind the sofa.
3. This elephant came from Africa.
4. The farmer was on his tractor.
5. My sister Sam was inside the flat.

● Write the six prepositions.

Unit 3 *Practice with poems and prose*

The pieces of writing on the next four pages are all about animals. They will give you a chance to practise writing smoothly. Try to write each poem or passage in one go, keeping the writing evenly spaced.

Good writers take pride in writing well.

Copy the pieces of writing.
Remember to check your letters and joins.

The Worm

Today I saw a little worm,
Wriggling on his belly,
Perhaps he'd like to come inside,
And see what's on the telly.

by Spike Milligan

The Crocodile

How doth the little crocodile
Improve his shining tail,
And pour the waters of the Nile
On every golden scale!

How cheerfully he seems to grin,
How neatly spreads his claws,
And welcomes little fishes in
With gently smiling jaws!

by Lewis Carroll

Practice with poems and prose

The Lion Pride

A family of lions is called a pride. There are usually about ten lions in a pride. Female lions are called lionesses. The babies are called cubs.

Lions roar to tell other lions where they are. They are lazy and often sleep all day.

Lions live in Africa and India.

The Rhinoceros

The rhino is a homely beast,
For human eyes he's not a feast,
But you and I will never know
Why Nature chose to make
him so.

by Ogden Nash

How are you getting on?
Look at the checklist.
Keep practising!

Unit 4 *Joining consonants* – ff, ll, ss

All these words contain double consonants (ff, ll or ss).
Double consonants often come at the end of a word.

ff   bluff cliff cuff offer staff
ll   fall holly spell tell yellow
ss   boss cross brass miss press

- Copy the words above and underline the double consonants.

- Now copy these sentences.
  Underline the double consonants.

The wolf was very cross. He said, "I'll huff and I'll puff and I'll blow your house down."

scr, spl, spr, str

Four of these words contain triple consonants.
Triple consonants usually come at the beginning of a word.

For tea there was scrumptious strawberry jam spread on splendid scones.

The three consonants blend together to make a special sound.

Copy these words and underline the triple consonants.

scr   scrap   scramble   scratch
      scream   scribble   scrub

spl   splash   splint   split   splatter
      splay   splodge   splinter

spr   spray   sprain   spring
      sprat   sprig   spree   spruce

str   straight   strange   strap
      street   stroll   strip

Unit 5   Vowel digraphs

A vowel digraph is two vowels put together.
We use the first and the third joins to make vowel digraphs.

b<u>oa</u>t   r<u>ai</u>n   s<u>ea</u>t   b<u>ee</u>

In the words on this page, the vowel digraph sounds like the name of the first vowel.

Copy these words.
Think about the sounds and how they are spelled.

oa   coach float foam goal loaf oat roast soap

ai   maid paint grain sail saint snail trail train

ee   deep knee queen sheep street three week wheel

ea   clean dream heal leaf meat please season team

e<u>i</u>ght　th<u>ie</u>f　c<u>oi</u>n　st<u>oo</u>l

b<u>oo</u>k　m<u>ou</u>se　gl<u>ue</u>

In the words on this page, the vowel digraph makes a special sound.

Copy these words.
Think about the sounds and how they are spelled.

ei　neighbour reign sleigh weigh

ie　believe field niece piece

oi　join point noise voice

oo (long)　boot choose food tooth

oo (short)　hood brook foot shook

ou　ground house sound south

ue　blue hue Sue true

Unit 6 Practice with all the joins – Silent letters

gnat — silent g

knot — silent k

A silent letter is part of the spelling of a word, but we don't hear it when we say the word.

- Make a chart like this with a column for each silent letter.

g	k	w	h	b
gnat	knot	wren	why	comb

- Think about the silent letter in each of these words.
  Write each word in the correct column.

knock wrist what crumb gnaw
lamb kneel sign when wrap
know whip wring numb gnash

14

ch

All these words contain *ch*. Sometimes it comes at the beginning of the word, sometimes in the middle and sometimes at the end.

choir   machine   touch

Say these words aloud. Can you hear the different sounds of *ch*?

Copy these sentences.
Underline all the *ch* words.

1. The chef had toothache.
2. An architect designed our school.
3. A mechanic helped the chauffeur start the car.
4. The chimney sweep caused chaos in the room.

Make a chart like this.

choir	machine	touch

Write each of the *ch* words in the correct column.

Unit 7 — Practice with verbs and adverbs

A verb is a word that shows action.
An adverb is a word that often tells how the action happened.

This is the verb.   This is the adverb.   Many adverbs end in *ly*.

He walked quickly to the station.

Copy these sentences.
Underline the verbs once.
Underline the adverbs twice.

1. The policeman blew his whistle loudly and started to run.
2. The express train thundered quickly past.
3. We listened carefully to Mr. Hill.
4. My tooth was aching badly.

Copy these sentences. Underline the adverbs. Do the adverbs tell you how, when or where the action happened? Write the words. The first three have been done for you.

Sometimes an adverb tells us when or where the action happened.

1. The goalkeeper dived <u>fearlessly</u> on the ball. (how)
2. We helped our mother <u>yesterday</u>. (when)
3. The angry crowd waited <u>outside</u>. (where)
4. He carefully carried the tray of glasses.
5. The dog ate his food hungrily.
6. The newspaper shop opens daily.
7. I looked everywhere for my key.

How are you getting on? Look at the checklist. Keep practising!

17

Unit 8 — Practice with conjunctions – and

A conjunction is used to join two simple sentences together to make one sentence.

and

He was tall. He had long legs.
He was tall and he had long legs.

Use the conjunction *and* to join each pair of sentences. Write the new sentences.

1. London is a big city.
   It is the capital of England.
2. Charlotte is a neat writer.
   She is also good at maths.
3. The new striker is very fast.
   He has a powerful kick.

but

but

When the two simple sentences contain opposite ideas, we use *but* instead of *and*.

James likes listening to the piano. He hates the violin.

James likes listening to the piano but he hates the violin.

Choose *and* or *but* to join each of these pairs of sentences. Write the new sentences.

1. I went to bed early.
   I could not sleep.

2. I arrived at the station on time.
   I got a seat on the train.

3. She wanted a bath.
   There was no hot water.

Unit 9 — Questions and answers

When you write a sentence which asks a question, you must always put a question mark (?) at the end.

What is your favourite meal?
My favourite meal is pizza.

? ? ? ? ? ? ? ? ? ? ? ? ? ? ? ? ?

- Practise writing question marks.

- Three of these five sentences ask questions.
Copy the three questions and add the question marks.

1. May I borrow your pencil sharpener.
2. Are those your new trainers.
3. I wish I could run faster.
4. How many is seven times six.
5. I lost my football in the bushes.

How are you getting on?
Look at the checklist.
Keep practising!

Think of a question to go with each of these answers.
The first one has been done for you.
Write the questions and answers.

1. How old were you when you started school?
   <u>I started school when I was five years old.</u>
2. No, I have never been to France.
3. Yes, you may borrow my camera.
4. No, blue is not my favourite colour.
5. King Harold was killed by an arrow.
6. Cinderella lost her slipper on the steps of the palace.
7. Jason is my best friend.

Don't forget the question marks.

Unit 10 Inverted commas

Inverted commas (speech marks) are used to enclose somebody's spoken words when we are reporting them in writing.

Mum said, "Let's go and see a film today."

" " " " " " " " " " " "

- Practise writing inverted commas.
- Copy these two sentences.
Remember the punctuation, including the inverted commas.

The football supporter shouted, "Come on, you reds."

The fairy godmother said, "I grant you three wishes."

Sometimes the name of the speaker begins the sentence.
Sometimes it comes at the end.
Copy these sentences, putting in the inverted commas.

1. Dad whispered, Please be quiet because the baby is asleep.
2. I would love an ice cream, said Tom.
3. Are we going swimming today? asked Kelly.
4. The waiter asked, What would you like to order?
5. That programme was really awful, cried Claire.
6. The captain called out, Fasten your seatbelts and get ready for take-off.

Unit 11 *Writing with a slope*

Sloping your joined writing slightly to the right will help you to write more quickly. To slope your writing correctly you need to position the paper like this.

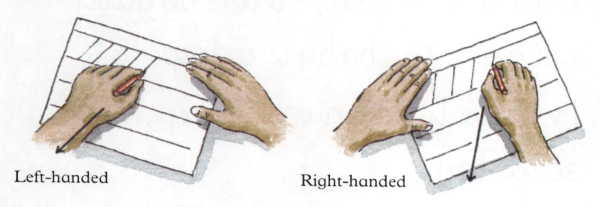

Left-handed   Right-handed

I always try to write well.

Practise these patterns and letters.
Try to slope them evenly to the right.

vvv vvv vvv vvv

uu uu uu uu

mmmm mmmm mmmm

dada dada dada dada

a b c d e f g h i j k l m

n o p q r s t u v w x y z

Look at this poem.
The first verse is in upright writing, and the second is in sloped writing.

People

Some people talk and talk
and never say a thing.
Some people look at you
and birds begin to sing.

Some people laugh and laugh
and yet you want to cry.
Some people touch your hand
and music fills the sky.

by Charlotte Zolotov

Now copy the sloping verse carefully, and then use a ruler to check that your slope is even.

Some people

The joins in sloped writing are exactly the same as they are in the upright writing you have learned.

Writing with a slope

Read these descriptions of unusual attempts to fly, and copy them carefully in sloped writing.

You need to practise so that you can slope your writing evenly.

Long ago in Persia, a king had the idea of tying a chair to four eagles. The eagles were to be steered by holding pieces of meat in front of their beaks.

Around the year 1,000 AD, a monk called Eilmer jumped off the tower of Malmesbury Abbey, wearing home-made wings.

Over three hundred years ago a man called Samuel Pepys kept a diary about events in London. These two entries are about the Great Plague and the Fire of London.

June 7th This day I did in Drury Lane see two or three houses marked with a red cross upon the doors and "Lord have mercy upon us" writ there, which was a sad sight to me.

September 2nd Jane called us up about three in the morning, to tell us of a great fire they saw in the City. So I rose and slipped on my nightgown and went to her window.

How are you getting on? Look at the checklist. Keep practising!

Copy these two diary entries carefully.
Think of an interesting event in the past and write a diary entry about it.

27

Unit 12 Vocabulary practice – Synonyms

dish bowl hurry rush

Words which have the same or similar meanings are called synonyms.

Find the synonyms.
Write the pairs of words.

quick   new
copy   habit
stop   hole
custom   steed
gap   imitate
lean   hard
modern   rapid
difficult   halt
horse   thin

Don't forget to slope your writing.

Antonyms

long   short   float   sink

Words which have opposite meanings are called antonyms.

Find the antonyms.
Write the pairs of words.

live   weak
bad   divide
strong   shallow
cheap   sell
deep   true
buy   expensive
false   good
dry   die
multiply   wet

Unit 13 Dictionary skills – Alphabetical order

A dictionary will help you to check your spelling. The words are arranged in alphabetical order.

a b c d e f g h i j k l m n o p q r s t u v w x y z

Write these words in alphabetical order.

First letter order

glacier wheat maize regular
above elephant handbag complete
jigsaw dense panda oyster

Second letter order

angry agree azure arch
above asleep adult awake
alarm aim atlas axle

Use your dictionary regularly. Practise finding words quickly.

Definitions

A dictionary will also help you to find out what a word means. This is called the definition of the word.

summit – the highest point of a mountain

Write each of these words next to its definition.
Use a dictionary to check your work.

> despair   revolve   inspect
> postpone   explode

to look carefully at something
to put off to another time
to blow up with a loud bang
to give up hope
to turn round in a circle

Unit 14 Speed writing

Legible writing is clear and easy to read.

Sometimes you may need to write more quickly than usual, for instance, when taking down a telephone message. The writing must be legible although you don't need to use your best writing.

Chris answered the telephone when Grandma telephoned with a message for Mum and Dad. Chris wrote down as much as there was time for.

> I will catch the ten o'clock train on Saturday, arriving at a quarter past twelve. Please meet me because I have hurt my back and cannot manage to carry my suitcase.

Chris could have shortened some of the words like this. Notice how an apostrophe is used when some of the letters have been left out.

I will – I'll
ten o'clock – 10.00
Saturday – Sat
arriving – arr
quarter past twelve – 12.15
Please – pl
I have – I've
cannot – can't
suitcase – case

Practise writing apostrophes.
They are like commas, but placed higher up.

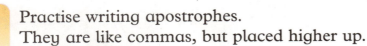

Copy the telephone message quickly, using the abbreviations listed.

33

Speed writing

Sometimes you may need to make notes about something you have read. Again, you don't need to use your best writing but make sure your writing is legible.

- Read this passage.

In 1877 a special boat was built. It was 23m long and was made of iron. It had no engine or sails and it was called the Iron Tube. It was made to carry "Cleopatra's Needle", an ancient Egyptian obelisk which was towed behind a ship from Egypt to London. The obelisk still stands beside the River Thames.

- A child made these notes as she read the passage.

> built 1877 23m long iron no engine or sails
> towed behind ship Egypt to London
> obelisk still beside R Thames

- Copy these notes, writing quickly but legibly.

- Now read the information below and make some quick notes about it.

In the 1930s a very odd ship was seen on the River Seine in Paris. The top was like a car and the bottom was made of two floats. Each float contained spiral fins which could spin round in the water. The car engine was used to drive the fins round, moving the ship through the water at quite high speeds.

Have you shortened any of the words?
Is your writing legible?

Unit 15 Drafting and editing

The way we write depends on what we are writing and on who is going to read it.

Tom wanted to write down his favourite recipe to give to a friend. He wrote a rough draft of the list of ingredients. He didn't use his best writing because nobody else was going to read it. Tom then edited and corrected his draft ready to do a final copy.

chocolate
Nests of ˰ eggs

grams   *margarine*
50 g of ~~margerine~~

2   *golden syrup*
~~Two~~ tablespoons of ~~gold syrup~~

tablespoons drinking chocolate
4 ~~tab~~ of ~~dr~~ choc

rice
2 tablespoons of ~~rise~~ crispies

Some chocolate mini - eggs

Some paper cake cases

Make a final copy of the list of ingredients for Tom.
Use your best writing, so that other people can read it.

Tom wrote each step of the recipe on a separate piece of paper for his friend. He used his best writing. He got the pieces of paper in the wrong order:

Spoon the mixture into the cake cases and make nest shapes.

Melt the margarine into a saucepan. Add the golden syrup.

When the mixture has set, fill each nest with mini-eggs.

Stir in the drinking chocolate. Add the rice crispies and mix it all together.

Write the recipe neatly in the correct order.

How are you getting on? Look at the checklist. Keep practising!

Unit 16 *Print*

When we write labels or fill in forms, we need to use print.
This means writing simple, unjoined letters like these.

Lower case print letters

a b c d e f g h i j k l m n
o p q r s t u v w x y z

Lower case letters for handwriting

a b c d e f g h i j k l m n
o p q r s t u v w x y z

Notice the difference between the print letters and the letters for handwriting. There are no flicks and f and k are different shapes.

- Write each print letter neatly three times.
  The capital letters and numerals are the same as for joined writing (see page 2).
  Copy each capital letter and each numeral twice.

- Labels on parcels are often printed.
  Copy these two labels carefully.

The Prime Minister
10 Downing Street
London SW1A 2AA

Thomas Nelson
Nelson House
Mayfield Road
Walton-on-Thames
Surrey KT12 5PL

- Now print two more labels, one addressed to your school and one to your home.

We use print to label diagrams.

Draw a man and woman like these, and print the labels neatly.

When you are printing labels, the letters can be quite small.

Print

When we order things from a catalogue we need to print the order clearly.

If you don't print clearly you might get the wrong things!

This is a page from a catalogue.
Each item has a price and a reference number.

ITEM	REFERENCE NUMBER	PRICE (£)
Bead-making kit	21/2710	12.95
Tape recorder	21/1654	32.50
Football	30/2891	3.75
Tennis racket	30/4702	13.49
Tool set	45/3721	13.85
Calligraphy set	45/1126	15.50
Fountain pen	45/4218	5.99
Starter camera	45/2233	15.25

Draw three columns with a ruler.
Copy the list carefully.

Did you remember the reference numbers and the prices?

Surinder sent away for some of the things in the catalogue. Here is her order form.

NAME	Surinder Patel		
ADDRESS	31a South Street Banthorpe Eastshire EY5 4TA		
QUANTITY	ITEM	REF.NO.	PRICE (£)
1	Starter camera	45/2233	15.25
1	Tennis racket	30/4702	13.49
2	Fountain pens	45/4218	5.99
1	Bead-making kit	21/2710	12.95

Draw two forms like this with a ruler.
Copy Surinder's order carefully on the first form.
Now write an order for yourself. Choose five things from the catalogue, and print the details on the second form.

Did you remember to use print?

Unit 17 Writing in ink

Until now you have probably done most of your writing in pencil, although you may have used fibre-tipped and plastic-tipped pens as well. This unit will help you start writing in ink, perhaps with a fountain pen.

Here are a few simple rules that will help.

Writing with a nib usually makes people's writing look better!

1 Sit correctly at your table or desk. Position your paper or book correctly.

2 Hold the pen lightly and press very lightly on the paper.

3 Hold your pen at the correct angle and try not to twist or turn it as you write.

First, get used to your pen by experimenting. Do some scribbling exercises like this.

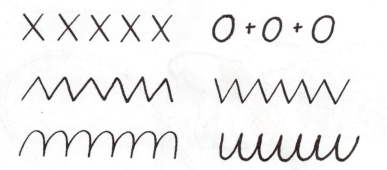

Now practise these exercises again until you can move your pen quickly and smoothly over the paper in any direction.

Try not to smudge your work by touching it when the ink is still wet. Use blotting paper if you need to turn a page.

Read the rules on page 42 again and then practise making these patterns quickly and smoothly.

Write this sentence several times.
Try to write smoothly with correct joins, gradually increasing your speed.

A pen should glide quickly and smoothly over the paper.

Does your pen glide easily over the paper?
Is there a clear space inside the letter *e*?

Now practise these exercises.

Writing in ink

A piece of writing will look really special if it is neatly written in ink and attractively presented.

- Copy this poem, taking care with your presentation.

I've Had This Shirt

I've had this shirt
that's covered in dirt
for years and years and years…

It used to be red
but I wore it in bed
and it went grey
'cos I wore it all day
for years and years and years…

by Michael Rosen

- Try to find and read the whole poem.

Now that you are getting used to managing your pen, you should practise frequently. Take care to slope your writing and remember the advice on page 42 as you copy this verse.
Think of an interesting way to present and illustrate it.

Winter Morning

Winter is the king of showmen,
Turning tree stumps into snowmen
And houses into birthday cakes,
And spreading sugar over the lakes.
Smooth and clean and frost white,
The world looks good enough to bite.
That's the season to be young,
Catching snowflakes on your tongue.

by Ogden Nash

Unit 18 Writing letters

When you write a letter, it has to be set out in a special way.

The name of the person who will read the letter

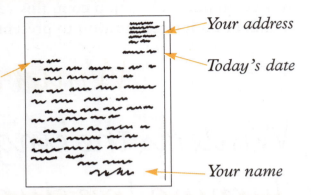

Your address

Today's date

Your name

Hannah's class was doing a project on teeth.
When Hannah read this verse of a poem by Pam Ayres, she decided to write to her dentist.

Oh, I Wish I'd Looked After me Teeth

Oh, I wish I'd looked after me teeth,
And spotted the perils beneath
All the toffees I chewed
And the sweet sticky food,
Oh, I wish I'd looked after me teeth.

by Pam Ayres

 Copy the poem and add a decorative border.

46

This is the letter Hannah wrote.
Copy the letter, taking care how you set it out.

> Year 4,
> Anytown Primary School,
> Anytown
> October 17th 1997
>
> Dear Mr. Fillit,
>
> Our class is learning about teeth. We read a poem by Pam Ayres. It made us think about how we should take care of our teeth.
>
> Could you let us have some leaflets or posters to help us with our project, please?
>
> Yours sincerely,
> Hannah Vitty

The dentist sent Hannah's class some leaflets and posters.
Write a thank you letter to the dentist.

How well have you done?
Look at the checklist.

Unit 19 Check your writing

- Copy these patterns.

You have come to the end of Pupil Book 2. This is a good time to check your writing.

- Copy this rhyme in your best handwriting.

Thirty days have September,
April, June and November.
All the rest have thirty-one,
Except February alone,
Which has twenty-eight days clear,
And twenty-nine in each leap year.

- Write this sentence legibly as many times as you can in two minutes.

We went for a walk in the park.